TABLE OF CON W9-DCX-469

A New True Book

MONARCH BUTTERFLIES

By Emilie U. Lepthien

CHILDRENS PRESS®
CHICAGO

Some monarch butterflies
winter in California.

PHOTO CREDITS
© Jerry Hennen—25, 26, 29 (right), 32 (left), 35
Journalism Services:
  © Mike Kidulich—37 (left)
  © Harvey Moshman—45
© Emilie Lepthien—43 (right)
Root Resources:
  © Ted Farrington—16 (left), 22, 33 (2 photos)
  © Conrad A. Gutraj—29 (left)
  © Glenn Jahnke—23
  © Earl L. Kubis—37 (right), 40 (right)
  © Don & Pat Valenti—40 (left)
Tom Stack & Associates:
  © Em Ahart—12
  © Hal Clason M.—2
  © W. Perry Conway—18, 44
  © Jeff Foott—7, 11 (2 photos), 43 (left)
  © Bob & Miriam Francis—13
  © John Gerlach—Cover
  © Don & Esther Phillips—14, 32 (right)
  © Ron Planck—24
  © John Shaw—15, 20, 31 (3 photos)
Lynn Stone—4, 9, 16 (right), 39

*To Vivian Norris whose friendship
I have cherished for almost a lifetime.*

Library of Congress Cataloging-in-Publication Data

Lepthien, Emilie U. (Emilie Utteg)
  Monarch butterflies / by Emilie U. Lepthien.
    p.   cm. — (A New true book)
  Includes index.
  Summary: Describes the physical characteristics
and habits of the Monarch, the only butterfly to migrate
for the winter.
  ISBN 0-516-01165-0
  1. Monarch butterfly—Juvenile literature.
[1. Monarch butterfly. 2. Butterflies.]
I. Title.
QL561.D3L47 1989   89-456
595.78′9—dc19   CIP
                                                AC

MONARCHS ARE VERY SPECIAL

Monarch butterflies are very special. Millions of monarchs are found throughout the United States and southern Canada in summer.

In mid-September millions of monarchs that live east of the Rocky Mountains migrate, or travel, thousands of miles to Mexico. They move in great flocks. No other butterflies migrate like the monarchs. It takes them two months to reach their winter home about seventy-five miles from Mexico City.

The monarchs' hideaway is high in the mountains. It was discovered by scientists in the mid-1970s. The people of Mexico had

A steer grazes in a carpet of monarch butterflies in Mexico.

known of the site for generations. Monarch butterflies had been shown in the artwork and embroidery done by the Indians since before the time of Columbus.

HOW AND WHY DO MONARCHS MIGRATE?

How do the monarchs find their way to their winter home and back north again? No one knows. Perhaps they use the position of the sun in the sky as a guide. Perhaps they have a kind of built-in compass. Scientists are trying to solve the puzzle.

No one knows why the

monarchs migrate. Some
scientists think they were
once tropical butterflies.
After the Ice Age they may
have followed their favorite
food—the milkweed plant—
as it spread farther north.

Monarch butterfly (in front) on milkweed plant

We do know that monarchs cannot stand cold weather. They need just the right temperature, sunlight, and humidity. They need protection from rain. They find all of these things in the Mexican mountains.

During the winter the butterflies feed on nectar, or sweet juices, from flowers. They store up energy for the long flight back north.

At night they rest in
trees. A tree may be
completely covered with
the beautiful butterflies.
The monarchs that live

west of the Rocky
Mountains also migrate.
But their journey is shorter
and not as amazing.
Thousands upon thousands
find a winter home near
the coast of southern
Oregon. Others fly to
California and as far south
as Mexico's Baja Peninsula.

THE BEAUTIFUL MONARCH

Monarch butterflies are beautiful. Their wings are orange and gold and brown. Black veins streak their wings. Their wing

span is four inches wide.
Even in their larva, or
caterpillar, stage, they are
colorful. The caterpillar's
skin is marked with bright
bands of yellow, green,
white, and black.

Monarchs look weak, but
they are strong.

Close-up of the scales

Each monarch has two pairs of wings. The wings are covered with dust-fine scales. The scales overlap like shingles on a roof.

These scales can shed rain. However, monarchs

Monarchs hang upside down (left). Can you see
the tiny hooks on their legs (right)?

prefer to avoid rain. They
find shelter on the
underside of a leaf or
branch. Tiny hooks on the
ends of their legs hold the
butterflies tightly as they
hang upside down.

When the sun comes out, the monarchs spread their wings to dry them. Like all butterflies, they have no way to warm their bodies except in the sun.

In late April or early May the monarchs begin their migration north from Mexico. Their flight is slow and lazy. Sometimes they seem almost to float on the breeze. They stop to eat along the way.

THE NEXT GENERATION OF MONARCHS

As they fly north, the monarchs mate. The females are attracted by a scent, or smell, released by the males.

After mating, the female monarch finds soft, tender milkweed leaves on which to lay her eggs. She lays one sticky, pale green egg on the underside of the milkweed leaf. In the warm

Egg on a milkweed leaf

sun the egg dries quickly
and sticks to the leaf. The
female lays just one egg
on each leaf.

The monarchs continue
their journey north. The
females lay eggs along
the way, just one egg on
each leaf. Each female
lays about 300 eggs.

THE LIFE CYCLE OF THE MONARCH

Like other butterflies, the monarch has four stages in its life cycle. The egg is the first stage. In the second stage, the larva, or caterpillar, hatches. In the third stage, the larva changes into a pupa, or chrysalis. Finally, the beautiful adult butterfly emerges. This is the fourth stage.

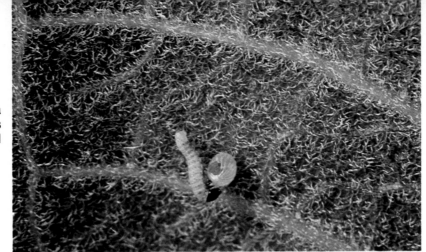

Larva eating its egg shell

THE MONARCH ENTERS THE LARVA STAGE

The eggs hatch in three to five days. Out of each monarch egg will come a tiny larva, or caterpillar. It will be only one eighth of an inch long. The caterpillar will eat its eggshell first.

Can you see the three pairs of legs near the head?

When each egg hatches, the caterpillar will have a milkweed leaf all to itself.

The monarch caterpillar has, eight pairs of legs. It uses five pairs to hold up its body when it crawls. These legs have hooks that hold the caterpillar to its leaf.

The other three pairs of legs are near the head.

These legs help the
caterpillar crawl. A pair of
black horns develops near
its head.

The caterpillars eat a
great deal. With the sharp

Caterpillars neatly eat leaves of milkweed plants.

nippers in their jaws, they
cut holes in the leaves.

They eat so much that
in a very few days they
are too big for their skins.
They must shed their old
skins.

On its lower lip each
monarch caterpillar has a
body part called a

spinneret. With it the
caterpillar can spin a
sticky, silky thread. The
caterpillar moves back and
forth on the leaf. It spins a
sticky carpet of threads.

The caterpillar stretches
out on the silky carpet

and hooks onto it. It rests while a new skin forms under the old one.

Finally the caterpillar puffs up until the old skin splits near its head. It pulls its way out of the old skin head first. Then it turns around and eats the old skin.

The caterpillar sheds its skin four times as it grows and grows.

THE CHRYSALIS IS FORMED

In two to three weeks the caterpillar is two inches long. It has shed its skin four times. Now it is time to find a place to enter its next stage—the pupa, or chrysalis.

The caterpillar looks for a firm branch or log. Then it spins a pad of silky threads on the underside of the log or branch. This

The caterpillar spins a silky pad (left) and then hooks onto it with its back feet (above).

place will protect the chrysalis from the weather.

The caterpillar spins a small knob on the silky pad. It hooks its back feet into the knob and hangs with its head down. The

caterpillar must hang
upside down to develop
into a chrysalis.

Soon the caterpillar
splits its larva skin for the
last time.

The skin splits upward
from the head to the tail.
The caterpillar must be
careful to slip out of the
old skin without falling off
the hanger.

The caterpillar is now

 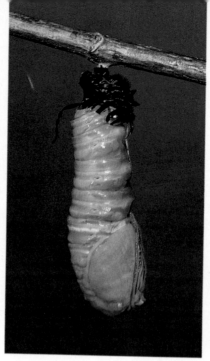 

Slowly, but surely, the caterpillar changes into a chrysalis.

becoming a chrysalis, or pupa. Its new skin is soft and damp. When the new skin dries, it is hard. It is a shiny green with gold dots.

Inside the chrysalis changes are taking place.

Inside the chrysalis
the butterfly's body
develops in twelve days.

In a week the colors of
the wings begin to show.
The wings and legs of
the adult butterfly are
developing. In twelve days
the shiny skin of the
chrysalis will split.

SAVING THE MONARCHS

The monarchs were in
danger by the time the
scientists found their
winter home. Trees were
being cut down. Farmers
began to plant crops. The
cutting of the trees and
planting of crops changed
the land. The temperature
of the area where the
monarchs wintered
became warmer during the

day and colder at night. These changes threatened the monarchs.

However, the local people needed the money from the trees that were cut. A sawmill operated in one of the densest monarch colonies.

Tourists invaded the monarchs' winter home. They came to see the masses of butterflies. They, too, harmed the butterflies by disturbing the colonies.

Warning signs (left) protect the monarchs. Tagging programs (above) allow scientists to track monarch butterflies.

The Mexican government knew something had to be done. It bought the sawmill and tore it down. It hired the tree cutters as guides.

Paths were made for the tourists. Now the tourists

43

could go only where guides took them.

In August 1986, a Mexican presidential decree provided for "ecological preserves." No more tree cutting can be done where the monarchs winter. Perhaps now these amazing butterflies will be safe.

WORDS YOU SHOULD KNOW

caterpillar(CAT • ih • pill • er) — the larva, or wormlike, stage in the life of a butterfly

chrysalis(KRISS • ah • liss) — a hardened case that is the pupa stage in the life of a butterfly

destination(dess • tin • AY • shun) — the end of a journey; a goal

ecological preserve(eck • uh • LOJ • ih • kil prih • ZERV) — a place set aside to protect an animal or plant that is in danger from humans

fragile(FRAJ • ill) — not strong; easily broken

generation(jeh • ner • RAY • shun) — all the individuals born at about the same time; parents are one generation and children are the next

hideaway(HYDE • away) — a place where animals can hide from enemies or from bad weather

humidity(hyoo • MID • ih • tee) — the amount of moisture in the air

larva(LAR • vah) — the second, or wormlike, stage in the life cycle of a butterfly

life cycle(LYFE SY • kil) — the series of changes a plant or animal goes through from an egg to an adult

migrate(MY • grait) — to travel, usually for a long distance, to find more food or better weather conditions

mimic(MIM • ick) — to copy; to take on the appearance of something else

navigate(NAV • ih • gait) — to find one's way on a journey

nectar(NECK • ter) — sweet, sugary juices produced by flowers

pupa(PYOO • pah) — the third stage in the life cycle of a butterfly, in which the larva changes into an adult

spinneret(spin • er • RET) — a body part on the lip of a caterpillar, used to spin silky threads

tropical(TROP • ih • kil) — living in the warm countries south of the United States

unique(yoo • NEEK) — the only one of its kind

INDEX

About the Author

Emilie Utteg Lepthien earned a BS and MA Degree and certificate in school administration from Northwestern University. She taught third grade, upper grade science and social studies, was a supervisor and principal of Wicker Park School for twenty years. Mrs. Lepthien has also written and narrated science and social studies scripts for the Radio Council (WBEZ) of the Chicago Board of Education.

Mrs. Lepthien was awarded the American Educator's Medal by Freedoms Foundation. She is a member of Delta Kappa Gamma Society International, Illinois Women's Press Association, National Federation of Press Women, Iota Sigma Epsilon Journalism sorority, Chicago Principals Association, and active in church work. She has co-authored primary social studies books for Rand, McNally and Company and served as educational consultant for Encyclopaedia Britannica Films.